THE KID'S GUIDE TO SAN DIEGO

1st edition

Eileen Ogintz

gpp®
travel

Guilford, Connecticut

Thank you to all those in San Diego and elsewhere in California who helped me gather information for this book, especially the kids who lent their ideas at Dewey Elementary School in San Diego, Clover Avenue Elementary School, and Celerity Troika Charter School in Los Angeles. Special thanks too to older San Diego students Jamie Ballard and Ruben Guardado who talked to younger ones in and around San Diego, and to Melanie Yemma for fact-checking.

All the information in this guidebook is subject to change. We recommend that you call ahead to obtain current information before traveling.

To buy books in quantity for corporate use
or incentives, call **(800) 962-0973**
or e-mail **premiums@GlobePequot.com**.

Copyright © 2014 Eileen Ogintz

Editor: Amy Lyons
Project Editor: Lauren Brancato
Layout: Maggie Peterson
Text Design: Sheryl Kober
Illustrations licensed by Shutterstock.com

ISBN 978-1-4930-0152-1

Printed in the United States of America

Contents

1

Welcome to San Diego

Ready to have some fun in the

sun? San Diego promises that perfect combination of sunny, warm weather—all year long—and miles of beaches.

No wonder the kids who live here—and grown-ups too—like to play outside! They are into biking, skateboarding, surfing, sailing, playing ball—you name it. It is also no surprise that so many families come here to vacation, especially in the spring and the summer.

Got your bathing suit? You can swim, take a surfing lesson, snorkel, kayak, or sail. You can also camp under the stars, bike, and hike (maybe in Anza-Borrego Desert

DID YOU KNOW?

The USS *Midway* is 1,001 feet long and was home to 4,500 sailors at a time from just after World War II until the early 1990s. Today it's a landmark on the Embarcadero as well as an interactive museum (check out the jet fighter on deck!) where you may take a tour guided by former sailors. The USS *Midway* Museum at Navy Pier highlights San Diego's military history and pays tribute to the hundreds of thousands of sailors who served on board.

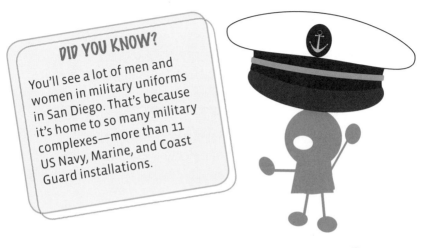

DID YOU KNOW?

You'll see a lot of men and women in military uniforms in San Diego. That's because it's home to so many military complexes—more than 11 US Navy, Marine, and Coast Guard installations.

State Park, the largest state park in California, or in Torrey Pines State Reserve in La Jolla). You'll find skate parks all over San Diego—and plenty of kids using them for skateboarding.

Of course, San Diego is more than its fantastic beaches. It's home to the world-famous San Diego Zoo, SeaWorld, LEGOLAND, and amazing museums like the New Children's Museum downtown that gives you a chance to create your own masterpieces. Exhibits here are often created *with* artists. Check out the building. It's downtown's first green project and was constructed with recycled materials.

San Diego is a good place to learn about California history—it is, after all, known as the birthplace of California. Practice your Spanish here. You can also get up close and personal with the sea life that calls the Pacific Ocean home—from the tiny creatures you'll see as you explore tide pools along the coast to the great gray whales offshore. You can see the whales every winter as they migrate south along the coast.

San Diego is made up of more than 100 different neighborhoods. You might visit:

- **The East Village,** home to Petco Park where the San Diego Padres play baseball.

- **The Gaslamp Quarter,** considered the heart of downtown. Did you know there were once three gambling halls here run by Wild West gunslinger Wyatt Earp?

DID YOU KNOW?

It doesn't rain often in San Diego. The city gets less than 12 inches of rain a year. Don't forget your sunscreen.

- **Little Italy,** where both locals and tourists come to eat.

- **Barrio Logan,** the center of San Diego's Hispanic community and the place to get great handmade tortillas and the city's best Mexican food.

- **Old Town San Diego,** where you can step back to the 1800s and see what life might have been like for you then. Try playing the games that the kids played!

A LOCAL KID SAYS:
"If you are coming to San Diego for the first time, you should know the beach is fun. My family goes every weekend."
—Bryan, 11

- **Mission Bay and the Beaches**, which is home not only to SeaWorld but also to a huge aquatic park where families swim, fish, fly kites, and go boating on all kinds of water vehicles.

- **Balboa Park,** which is called "The Smithsonian of the West" because it is home to 15 museums as well as the San Diego Zoo and theaters.

- **La Jolla,** famous for its beaches, the Museum of Contemporary Art San Diego, the Birch Aquarium, and plenty of places to play outdoors like Coronado—across San Diego Bay from downtown and known for its beaches and small-town vibe. Families have been coming here to vacation for more than 100 years!

- **Carlsbad,** home to LEGOLAND and fantastic beaches, including spots where you can camp right near the ocean. The calm waters here are great for boogie boarding!

- **Ocean Beach,** home to the famous Ocean Beach Pier, where you can try surfing, play beach volleyball, fish from the pier, or join hundreds of locals watching the huge waves break during a winter storm.

The hardest part will be deciding where to go first!

Ready to Time Travel?

Hop aboard the *Star of India,* the world's oldest merchant sailing vessel still in operation, and you're transported back 150 years. She was launched before Lincoln gave the Gettysburg Address! Come in summer and go for a sail aboard the *Californian,* a replica of the 1847 ship that patrolled the coast during the Gold Rush. There's an 1898 steam ferryboat from San Francisco Bay (during the 1906 San Francisco earthquake, her captain and crew helped ferry survivors). Check out the deepest diving submarine. You'll find those ships and more at the **Maritime Museum of San Diego** (1492 N. Harbor Dr.; 619-234-9153; sdmaritime.org).

DID YOU KNOW?

In San Diego Bay, you'll see all kinds of boats and ships—huge US Navy vessels, cruise ships, fishing boats, and sailing boats of all sizes. A great way to see San Diego Bay is to go on a harbor tour or a winter whale watching expedition.

Festival Fun!

No matter when you visit San Diego, you'll find special festivals:

January: Big Bay Whale Days help you learn about the annual winter migration of the California gray whales along the coastline here (whaledays.com).

February: You'll love the Lion and Dragon Dances at the **Annual Chinese New Year and Cultural Fair** (sdcny.org).

March: The **Spring Busker Festival** at Seaport Village even has street performers (seaportvillage.com). Have you ever seen a sword swallower?

May: The **Annual Old Town Fiesta Cinco de Mayo** celebrates everything Mexican (oldtownsandiegoguide.com).

July: A **Fourth of July** festival with fireworks takes place over the San Diego Bay; it is the largest fireworks display in the country (sandiego.org).

August: You can watch as more than 300 tons of sand is molded into amazing sculptures at the **US Sand Sculpting Challenge** (ussandsculpting.com).

October: The best military and civilian pilots in the world participate in the **MCAS Miramar Air Show** (miramarairshow.com).

December: Holiday lights with **Balboa Park December Nights** is the largest free festival in San Diego (balboapark.org), and the **San Diego Bay Parade of Lights** showcases more than 100 boats bedecked with lights sailing in San Diego Bay (sdparadeoflights.org).

Old Town and "New Town"

Get ready! You might meet some ghosts when you're exploring **Old Town San Diego State Historic Park** (parks.ca.gov). **Old Town,** of course, is San Diego's first "downtown," but more than that, it represents San Diego's Hispanic heritage from 1821 to 1872. That's when Mexico gained independence from Spain and took over here. You'll see Mexican shops, restaurants, museums, and adobe buildings spread out over the 6-block park. Check out the schoolhouse and blacksmith shop!

The **Gaslamp Quarter** (gaslampquarter.org), a 16-block area, is known as San Diego's "New Town" because in 1869 developer Alonzo Horton wanted to relocate downtown away from Old Town. He's considered the father of San Diego. You'll find lots of restaurants and shops—including the huge Westfield Horton Plaza. Got your souvenir money?

DID YOU KNOW?

San Diego's Little Italy was originally a fishing community in the 1800s. Now it is a place where people come to eat and shop.

Souvenir Smarts

Seaport Village and the Gaslamp Quarter are great places to buy souvenirs. Before you go souvenir hunting:

A LOCAL KID SAYS:
"Get a San Diego
lifeguard hoodie for a souvenir!"
—Rose, 11

- Talk to your parents about how much you can spend. Some families save loose change in a jar all year to spend on souvenirs!

- Consider if you want one big souvenir or several smaller things to add to a collection like pins, patches for your backpack, or stickers that you could put on your water bottle.

- Resist impulse buys and choose something that you can only find in San Diego.

DID YOU KNOW?

Old Town San Diego not only was San Diego's first downtown but also the first Spanish settlement on the West Coast (oldtownsandiego.org).

Old Town San Diego is considered the birthplace of California.

Staying Safe on Vacation

- Write down the name and phone number of the hotel where you are staying. Also write down your parents' phone numbers—or make sure they are in your phone. Carry these numbers with you wherever you go.

- Practice "what-if" situations with your parents. What should you do if you get lost in a museum? A theme park? On a city street?

- Only ask uniformed people for help if you get lost—police officers, firefighters, store security guards, or museum officials wearing official badges.

- Wherever you go, decide on a central and easy-to-locate spot to meet in case you get separated.

A LOCAL KID SAYS:
"My dad makes me bring sunglasses when I go somewhere outside in San Diego so I can see in case it is too bright."
—Melissa, 12

TELL THE ADULTS

There's a lot to do in and around San Diego that's free—or nearly free:

- During the entire month of October, families with children can enjoy special deals at San Diego hotels, restaurants, attractions, museums, and transportation companies during "Kids Free San Diego" Month. Providing families an opportunity to save during budget-conscious times, "Kids Free San Diego" Month offers a variety of "kids free" incentives ranging from complimentary meals and admission to attractions.

- Enjoy free organ concerts at 2 p.m. on Sunday at the **Spreckels Organ Pavilion** in Balboa Park. The Organ Pavilion features one of the world's largest outdoor pipe organs, a San Diego landmark since 1914, where organists play traditional favorites, waltzes, and show tunes on enormous 32-foot pipes.

- Both locations of the Museum of Contemporary Art San Diego (MCASD) are free for everyone under 25.

- Visit in February for half-off admission to 40 museums the entire month. Get a free Museum Month Pass at Macy's.

- Go to the beach! They're all free for swimming, playing in the sand, or collecting seashells.

- Window-shop at **Seaport Village** with more than 50 shops and lots of free entertainment (849 W. Harbor Dr.; 619-235-4014; seaportvillage.com).

- Fly a kite along the grassy field in **Mission Bay Park,** a 4,600-acre aquatic park (sandiego.org/discover/mission-bay-beaches.aspx).

- Wander free through Old Town's historic buildings, including the blacksmith shop, Seeley Stables, and the oldest schoolhouse in San Diego.

- Stargaze outside the **Reuben H. Fleet Science Center** in Balboa Park on the first Wednesday of every month. The San Diego Astronomy Association sets up huge telescopes to offer guests a great view of all the stars in the night sky (sandiego.org/members/museums/reuben-h-fleet-science-center.aspx).

- In-line skate, skateboard, or bike along the **Mission Beach Boardwalk**, a scenic 3-mile boardwalk along picturesque Mission and Pacific Beaches (sandiego .org/what-to-do/beaches/mission-beach.aspx).

- Go snorkeling and stay to watch the sun set at **La Jolla Cove,** the northernmost point on the seaward end of the cliffs (8200 Camino del Oro, La Jolla).

- Take a scenic walk along the **Big Bay,** San Diego's "largest attraction," with 27 miles of waterfront featuring bayside parks, marinas, hundreds of shops and restaurants, and miles of promenades and bikeways. Take a walk along the Embarcadero (thebigbay.com).

{ What's Cool? Riding with Sea and Land Adventures that go both on land and water and get you close up to the naval ships around San Diego Bay (sealtours.com).

CONNECT THE DOTS

You can see thousands of gray whales—the world's largest mammals—off the coast of San Diego as they make their way from Alaska to Baja December through April. In the fall and summer, you can spot humpback, fin, and minke whales, and dolphins too! Connect the dots to draw your own gray whale!

2

Balboa Park:

Fun Museums, Pretty Gardens & Famous Puppet Shows

Maybe you want to try a new

skateboarding trick. Maybe you want to stop and smell the roses or take a "selfie" surrounded by flowers. Maybe you want to see a puppet show or go to a museum that's got plenty of kid-tested activities. You can do all that and more in **Balboa Park** in San Diego (1549 El Prado; 619-239-0512; balboapark.org).

It's right in the heart of downtown San Diego and unlike any other park you've visited. That's because besides all the trees (there are 58 different species of palms!) and flowers, Balboa Park is home to the San Diego Zoo, 15 museums, the

A LOCAL KID SAYS:
"I like visiting the Balboa Park gardens in the spring when everything is in bloom. It's so amazingly beautiful!"
—Ellie, 15

Old Globe Theater, the Marie Hitchcock Puppet Theater, and the San Diego Junior Theatre.

Kids and their parents have been coming here for 100 years! If you think the buildings themselves along the park's famous El Prado pedestrian walkway are interesting, that was the idea when they were built during the Panama-California Exposition of 1915-16. They're built in what is called Spanish Revival style, which reflects San Diego's history. These were some of the first buildings of this style built in the country.

DID YOU KNOW?

The Spreckels Organ is the largest outdoor pipe organ in the world with 4,500 pipes in 72 ranks—the tallest is 32 feet high; the tiniest 6 inches (sosorgan.org). Come for a free Sunday concert!

Twenty years later, in 1935–36, more buildings were added around the Pan American Plaza at the south end of the park

for the California Pacific International Exposition. You'll see that these buildings are in a different style.

The park also showcases San Diego's ethnic diversity—from the **Centro Cultural de la Raza** exhibiting the art and culture of Mexicans, Chicanos, and Native Americans (centroculturaldelaraza.com) to the **Japanese Friendship Garden** with sushi making workshops on some weekends (niwa.org) to the **Spanish Village Art Center** housed in a Spanish-style village (spanishvillageart.com), and the **WorldBeat Cultural Center** that celebrates African culture (worldbeatcenter.org).

You'll want to ride the **Balboa Park Carousel** (can you catch the brass ring?) and take a short (just 3-minute) ride on the old-fashioned **Balboa Park Miniature Railroad.**

DID YOU KNOW?

San Diego Junior Theatre in Balboa Park is the oldest continuing theater program in the country (juniortheater.com). Kids love to see performances with kids and for kids!

There's plenty to learn—and fun to be had—at museums like the **San Diego Air & Space Museum** (so many planes on display!), the **San Diego Natural History Museum** (ready to explore fossils?), and the **Reuben H. Fleet Science Center** (the planetarium shows are terrific!).

Imagine yourself stepping into a painting at the San Diego Museum of Art, the Timken Museum of Art, or the San Diego Art Institute's Museum of the Living Artist.

But there's plenty more that you might not find elsewhere. Kids especially like:

- The scale models of the American Southwest at the **San Diego Model Railroad Museum** (1649 El Prado; 619-696-0199; sdmrm.org). Don't miss the interactive Toy Train Gallery. Your parents will like that the museum is free.

- **San Diego Hall of Champions** (2131 Pan American Plaza; 619-234-2544; sdhoc.com), where you can learn about how surfboards evolved into what they are today.

- The **San Diego Automotive Museum** (2080 Pan American Plaza; 619-231-2886; sdautomuseum.org) with all kinds of cars and motorcycles.

- The **San Diego Museum of Man** (1350 El Prado, Balboa Park; 619-239-2001; museumofman.org), where you can see what life was like for native Californians thousands of years ago and see the tools of a prehistoric handyman.

If only you had more time . . .

DID YOU KNOW?

William S. Harley was only 21 when he first drew up plans for a motor-bicycle, which of course later became Harley-Davidson motorcycles. That was back in 1901. You can hop aboard a motorcycle at the **San Diego Automotive Museum** in Balboa Park (sdautomuseum.org).

From Outer Space to Inside the Human Body

Would you rather journey inside a cell or into outer space?
The **Reuben H. Fleet Science Center in Balboa Park** (1875 El Prado; 619-238-1233; rhfleet.org) has more than 100 hands-on exhibits and Southern California's only IMAX Dome Theater. Let's not forget the simulator ride into outer space and the planetarium shows where you can take a Cosmic Journey. There are special workshops for kids and families too.

Use a microscope to examine human tissue or fly through a human cell. Reach through a twisting tornado. The idea is to use your senses—and your mind—and see what you can discover about the world around you.

At the Exploration Bar, check out the science experiments on electricity and magnetism, among other things. Find out if you can believe what you see in the Gallery of Illusions and Perceptions (not always!). Explore how your mind and your body sometimes work against each other!

Who says science isn't fun?

Water Smarts

In San Diego, more than 80 percent of the water is imported from the Colorado River and Northern California. Conserving water is one way we can help protect biodiversity and the places that supply our imported water. The changing climate has been impacting water supplies with prolonged drought. None of us can afford to waste water, especially in California. To learn more about the natural life that calls San Diego home, visit the Museum's Field Guides, developed by the San Diego Natural History Museum's Biodiversity Research Center of the Californias.

Here's how the San Diego Natural History Museum says you can help:

- Turn off the water when you brush your teeth.

- Take shorter showers and only fill the tub halfway if you want a bath instead.

- Don't use the toilet as a wastebasket (each flush uses 1.6 gallons of water!).

- Garden with plants that don't need a lot of water ... or grow food, not lawns.

- How you eat can save water—eat less meat and eat more unprocessed plant-based foods.

Blast Off! Fun Facts

- It's fitting that San Diego has such a great Air & Space Museum since this city is considered the birth-place of naval aviation.

A LOCAL KID SAYS:
"The Air & Space Museum is my favorite. The U Fly It exhibit is cool!"
—Riley, 12

- The earliest use of rockets we know of was by the Chinese in 1232, the San Diego Air & Space Museum says. They called them "fire arrows" and gunpow-der made them go.

- American Robert Goddard launched the first liquid-fueled rocket back in 1926, and a lot of people thought he was crazy to think people could fly to the moon.

- Today, of course, you can see an Apollo command module at the museum in Balboa Park as well as the planes that were flown by aviation pioneers—everything from sea-planes to warplanes. There are more than 60 aircraft.

- Try out a MaxFlight Simulator. Think you want to be a test pilot or an astronaut?

- You'll also learn the stories of aviation pioneers who have made today's air and space flight possible. Think of them the next time you're on a plane!

Star Lingo

We're talking about the language that astronomers use. Learn about astronomy at the **Reuben H. Fleet Science Center** (1875 El Prado; 619-238-1233; rhfleet.org) and the men and women who explore space at the **San Diego Air & Space Museum** (2001 Pan American Plaza; 619-234-8291; sandiego airandspace.org).

The first Wednesday of every month, the **San Diego Astronomy Association** (sdaa.org) sets up huge telescopes to offer guests a great view of all the stars in the night sky. Here are some of the things you'll learn:

- **Astronomy** is the study of space.

- The **atom** is the simplest building block of the universe.

- A **comet** is a small icy object from the outer part of the solar system.

- An **extraterrestrial** is any object, living or not, originating from someplace other than our planet.

- An **extremophile** is an organism that has adapted to survive in extreme environments, such as blazing hot or freezing cold conditions.

- A **galaxy** is a massive collection of stars and celestial objects bound together into a single system by gravity.

- Earth and our sun and its other planets are all part of the **Milky Way** galaxy.

- A **meteorite** is a stony or metallic object from space that survives a fiery entry into the earth's atmosphere and lands on the surface.

- A **solar system** is a group of planets, moons, asteroids, comets, and other small objects that orbit one star.

- The **sun** is the only star in our solar system.

TELL THE ADULTS

Valid for 7 consecutive days, the **Passport to Balboa Park** (balboapark.org) provides visitors with admission to 13 museums in Balboa Park including the San Diego Natural History Museum, the San Diego Museum of Art, Museum of Photographic Arts, Reuben H. Fleet Science Center, and more. The Passport costs $53 for adults and $29 for children. The Zoo/Passport Combo pairs the Passport to Balboa Park with 1-day "best value" admission to the San Diego Zoo including a 50-minute bus tour and Skyfari tram ride. The Zoo/Passport Combo costs $89 for adults and $52 for children. The Stay for the Day excursion pass for adults allows visits to five museums for $43.

DID YOU KNOW?

You can see 200 different kinds of roses at the big Inez Grant Parker Memorial Rose Garden in Balboa Park near the San Diego Natural History Museum. You might see a bride too—lots of couples come here to take their wedding pictures.

Museums are great places to learn, as well as have fun and meet local families. Here's how to make the most of your experience:

Take a virtual tour of the museum you plan to visit ahead of time. Because many museums are too big to see in a few hours, zero in on a few exhibits you want to see and don't worry about not exploring everything. You may find online games for the kids at the **California Science Center Fun Lab** (californiasciencecenter.org/FunLab/FunLab.php) that will help prepare them for what they are going to see.

Come when you are well rested and have eaten.

Wear comfortable shoes.

Look on the museum website or ask when you arrive to see if there are special family activities that day.

Stop at the museum gift shop when you arrive and get some postcards so you can have a scavenger hunt while you are there and stop on your way out for souvenirs.

SECRET WORD DECODER

Using the key, write the letters under the symbols to figure out the secret phrase. Clue: This ride goes around and around and around . . .

For example: 🚲 🛶 🏛 ✈ = b i r d

_ _ _ _ _ _ _ _ _ _ _ _ _ _

a= ✔   b= 🚲   c= 🏙   d= ✈   e= 🎁

f= 🏭   g= 🏛   h= 🏠   i= 🛶   j= 🏡

k= 🌿   l= ✦   m= ❗   n= 👁   o= 🛥

p= 🛤   q= 🌲   r= 🏛   s= ?   t= 🏟

u= 📢   v= 🔶   w= ⚑   x= ◀   y= ♥

z= 🌾   .= ◼   != 🚌   ,= 🌶

See page 153 for the answers.

NOW TRY AND MAKE YOUR OWN SECRET
MESSAGES IN THE SPACE BELOW.

3

The San Diego Zoo &
Wild Safari Park:

Pandas, Koalas &
a Real Safari

What's your favorite animal?

There is a good chance you'll find it—and a lot you have never seen—at the **San Diego Zoo** and its **Safari Park**. Have you ever seen a pygmy hippopotamus or a California condor?

There are 3,700 animals to see, representing some 650 species. The Safari Park has more than 2,600 animals representing more than 300 species.

That's a lot more than lions and tigers and bears, though you'll find them here too, of course. It's a good idea to take a virtual tour to decide with your family what you want to see before you come. That way everyone gets to spend time with some of his or her favorite creatures. The zoo's website even has

A LOCAL KID SAYS:
"We got to pet the giraffes at the Safari Park."
—Jarrad, 12

a handy **Animal Finder** (zoo.sandiegozoo.org/animals) to find your favorite animal by the "zone" where it lives.

Do you have comfy shoes and a water bottle? You'll be glad you've got both as you explore. The zoo is big!

Of course you'll want to see the giant pandas at **Panda Canyon.** There aren't many zoos that have them. Aren't they cute—especially the baby!

You'll also want to see the koalas at the **Outback.** Did you know the San Diego Zoo has the largest koala colony outside of Australia? Practice your own koala-climbing skills on the play structure with life-size koala sculptures. How do you measure up size-wise? Check out the laughing kookaburra and the Tasmanian devil. Make sure you've got your camera handy!

The San Diego Zoo is famous for creating habitats for the animals that look like where they would live in the wild—whether they are koalas, pandas, elephants, or the hippos you'll see through an underwater viewing window as they play in the water. Looks like fun! Along the Tiger Trail, you'll think you are in a rain forest with all the strange trees and plants.

Head to the **Polar Bear Plunge** and watch them take a dive (there's an underwater viewing area here too) and spend the time to learn about how climate change is impacting their survival. There are interactive games to try.

You can pet the goat and sheep at the **Children's Zoo** and, if you're lucky, see the babies being bottle-fed. You also won't want to miss:

- The **Lost Forest** where the orangutans swing through the trees and you can see some of the rarest monkeys

DID YOU KNOW?

Some of the Galapagos tortoises at the San Diego Zoo are more than 100 years old. They weigh just a few ounces when they're born but can grow to be 500 pounds!

in the world. Walk at treetop level to watch them along the Monkey Trails. Watch the colobus monkeys burp. That's how they say hi to each other!

- The enclosed aviaries where strange birds fly by your face.

- **Africa Rocks** where you can meet a snow leopard, among other creatures.

- **Discovery Outpost** for snakes, Komodo dragons, and the giant Galapagos tortoise.

- The **Northern Frontier** where besides the polar bears you can get face-to-face with arctic fox and reindeer.

- The **Urban Jungle** that's home to the giraffe and cheetah.

- The **Asian Forests** where you'll meet bears playing.

- **Elephant Odyssey** where along with the elephants are lions, jaguars, and the California condor.

Wow! You've traveled around the world—without leaving San Diego.

Got a new favorite animal?

{ **What's Cool?** Climbing and swinging like a monkey through the trees on a Jungles Ropes Safari at the San Diego Zoo Safari Park (sdzsafaripark.org).

Humans Are Mammals!

The San Diego Zoo experts tell us there are more than 4,000 species of mammals—including humans. These range from tiny hog-nosed bats who weigh just a few hundredths of an ounce to giant blue whales who weigh 150 tons.

But we all share some things:

- We all have a backbone or spine. That means we're vertebrates.

- We're all warm-blooded. Because we can regulate our body temperatures, we live in almost every climate.

- We have hair.

- We produce milk to feed our babies.

Going on Safari without Leaving San Diego

You can do that when you visit the **San Diego Zoo Safari Park,** about 35 miles from the downtown San Diego Zoo (15500 San Pasqual Valley Rd., Escondido; 760-747-8702; sdzsafaripark.org).

- There are cheetahs and warthogs, African lions and elephants, Sumatran tigers, Uganda giraffes, gorillas, even white rhinos. Let's not forget the birds—including the California condor at Condor Ridge. There may be animals you've never heard of!

- Take the **Africa Tram** around some of the exhibits.

- Get up close to cheetahs (safely!) and see them run as they race on a long track in the **Lion Camp.** You can even go up in a balloon over the Safari Park grounds—up 400 feet—or feed the lorikeets at Lorikeet Landing.

- Kids love the **Frequent Flyers Bird Show,** meeting "Robert," the interactive digital zebra, and talking to the elephant keepers. Don't miss the **Jameson Research Island**—that's really a water play area—and the **Samburu Jungle Gym.**

- Of course you've come to see the animals the way they live in the wild. You can even fly high across the park on a **zip line!** Most visitors take a cart safari. Would you rather go to Africa or Asia?

39

Panda Power

Ready to meet a celebrity? **Xiao Liwu** (pronounced like sshyaoww lee woo) was born in July 2012. The zoo's youngest giant panda has fans all over the world who watch him on the zoo's Panda Cam and keep track of his progress through video clips and blogs. The zookeepers call him Mr. Wu.

You might see him with his mom **Bai Yun** (by YOON), the zoo's adult female. Say hi to Gao Gao (Gow Gow), the adult male. Did you know they have air-conditioned bedrooms? The zookeepers even bake a kind of bamboo "bread" for Gao Gao because he has trouble with his teeth. That takes a lot of work!

- The pandas are on loan from China. Of the six pandas born at the San Diego Zoo, five now live in China.

- Giant pandas eat four our five different kinds of bamboo, and sometimes there isn't enough for them in the wild. They used to be able to move to another place when one area was stripped, but now humans take up a lot of their habitat.

- The zoo conservationists have helped increase the number of giant panda's in China's Wolong Breeding Center to more than 100—from just 25.

- Giant pandas have been loved, especially in China, for thousands of years. The Chinese call them "large bear-cats." Today only about 1,600 giant pandas survive, and scientists, including those from the San Diego Zoo, are working hard to help them keep going and thrive. They are tracking them in the wild to figure out how they find each other to breed, recording the sounds they make, and testing their hearing in the zoo. They're even studying the messages they may leave one another by their scents.

What have you learned about pandas at the zoo?

Zoo Talk

Here's the lingo that the San Diego Zoo says will help you understand the animals and their behavior. You can find an entire glossary at kids.sandiegozoo.org/glossary. How many are characteristics you have?

1 **ALARM SIGNAL**—the way animals communicate to alert each other to a predator

2 **ALPHA**—can be a male or female but is the strongest in a species in a small area

3 **ARBOREAL**—being able to live in trees, like a parrot

4 **AQUATIC**—being able to live in water, like a turtle

5 **BIPEDAL**—moving around on two feet

6 **DIGITGRADE**—Walking on toes, like elephants

7 **FRUGIVORE**—fruit-eater

8 **CARNIVORE**—meat-eater

9 **GRANIVORE**—eating grain or seeds

10 **OMNIVORE**—eating all kinds of foods, both plants and animals—like most humans do

11 **JUVENILE**—a young animal still cared for by adults or even if able to care for itself; it isn't the size of an adult yet

12 **MARSUPIAL**—a type of mammal that develops in a pouch

13 **NOCTURNAL**—awake and active during the night; asleep during the day

14 **PEST**—a plant or animal that is believed to be harmful and/or annoying

15 **SANGUINIVORE**—an animal that drinks blood

A LOCAL KID SAYS:
"When I went to the Safari Park, monkeys climbed on my car. They threw fruit at each other and ate it!"
—William, 12

43

Endangered Species and How You Can Help

The San Diego Zoo is home to more than 4,000 rare and endangered animals. And it is dedicated to saving endangered species worldwide with more than 100 conservation projects in 35 countries. To date, these efforts have helped reintroduce 33 species back into the wild—reptiles, birds, and mammals.

You can help save endangered species when you adopt an animal at the San Diego Zoo. Choose an animal and for a small donation you will be the guardian of that species at the zoo for a year (sandiegozoo.org/adopt/animal.html).

Many other species are *threatened*, which means that unless conservation efforts are started, they're likely to become endangered. Animals and humans are part of one world with one ocean and it is up to us to protect them. Every day, you can do small, simple things to help the planet:

- Turn off lights when you leave a room.

- Turn off the television if no one is watching it.

- Create a recycling center in your home and recycle newspapers, glass, and aluminum cans.

- Turn off the water while brushing your teeth.

- Use both sides of a piece of paper.

- Plant wildflowers in your garden instead of picking them from the wild.

- Reduce the amount of trash you create: Reuse your lunch bag each day.

- Don't buy animals or plants taken illegally from the wild or that are not native to your area. Ask where they're from.

Share what you know with family and friends!

TELL THE ADULTS

The San Diego Zoo is big, spreading more than 100 acres and housing over 3,700 animals representing more than 650 species. It's also one of the most popular tourist attractions in San Diego, hosting millions of visitors every year.

Take a virtual tour before you visit to decide where you want to head first. Encourage the kids to visit the Zoo and Safari Park's Kid Site (kids.sandiego zoo.org). Have a talk in advance about what—if any—souvenirs they will want to buy.

Come in October. For the entire month, kids get in free. The rest of the year, you can purchase 1-day passes, passes that enable you to visit both the Zoo and the Safari Park. If you think you will want to visit more than once, consider becoming a member, and you will get free unlimited admission to both the San Diego Zoo and the San Diego Zoo Safari Park along with other discounts. It doesn't cost much more than onetime admission to both the Zoo and Safari Park.

You can also get the **GO San Diego card** that gives you all-inclusive discounted admission to all 45 San Diego attractions, though you must use it within 3 days (smartdestinations.com/san-diego-attractions-and-tours). If you plan to visit other Southern California attractions, consider a CityPASS, which also includes admission to the Disney parks (citypass.com).

To enhance your visit, sign on for a special tour (zoo.sandiegozoo.org/experiences).

The **Backstage Pass** lets you get up close with many animals.

You can even **spend the night at the zoo**—complete with early morning animal viewing.

The **Inside Look Tour** is a 2-hour immersion tour in how the animals are cared for.

The **Exclusive VIP Experience** takes you off-exhibit with unique animal interactions.

Have the zoo to yourself after dark and take a **Twilight Trek** to see what animals do at night or come early certain Saturdays and Sundays at 7:30 am, before the zoo opens for a 90-minute **Sunrise Stroll**.

Who Takes Care of the Animals?

It takes a lot of people with a lot of different skills to take care of the animals at the San Diego Zoo and Safari Park. They include:

The **zookeeper** who feeds and takes care of the animals in specific areas.

A **horticulturist** who takes care of all the plants and the trees that provide shelter and food for the animals.

A **nutritionist** who makes sure the animals are eating the right mix of food.

A **veterinarian** who treats illnesses and makes sure the animals stay healthy.

Lab technicians who do all kinds of tests on samples taken from the animals in the laboratories.

{ **What's Cool?** Meeting up with members of the teen Zoo Corps at their discovery stations throughout the zoo. They'll teach you all about the animals you are meeting!

CAN YOU FIND YOUR WAY THROUGH THE SAFARI?

4

SeaWorld:

Shamu, Roller Coasters & a Huge Water Playground

Feeling the need to get wet?

Head to SeaWorld's famous **Splash Zone** at Shamu
Stadium. You're guaranteed to be soaked as the Shamu
family of whales, including Baby Shamu, strut their stuff
swimming and leaping. Watch the older whales teaching
the younger ones! As you enter the park, check out the
new **Explorer's Reef** where you can touch shark pups,
rays, horseshoe crabs, and more.

    SeaWorld San Diego (500 Sea World Dr.; 619-226-3901;
seaworldsandiego.com) is the place to get up close to
whales, dolphins (check out the Dolphin Point), and sea
lions (everybody thinks they're really funny at the Clyde
and Seamore Show)—and at Otter Outlook you can meet
California sea otters taken in by SeaWorld.

DID YOU KNOW?

Sea lion colonies are noisy
places because sea lions often
call loudly to each other. You
can hear them bark and see
them swim, dive, and jump at
the funny sea lion and otter
show at SeaWorld.

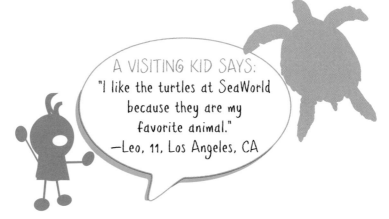

The sharks and tropical fish swim over and under you as you walk through a clear tunnel at the **Shark Encounter.**

Meet more than 40 threatened green sea turtles at Turtle Reef along with thousands of tropical fish. Did you know some of the turtles are more than 50 years old?

Birds join the whales and dolphins at the **Blue Horizons** show at the Whale and Dolphin Theater while dogs and cats take to the stage at **Pets Ahoy!** (Bet your pooch can't do these kinds of tricks!) *Madagascar* movie fans will want to see Madagascar Live! Operation: Vacation.

{ What's Cool? Watching sharks and tropical fish swim all around you as you are in a long acrylic tube underwater at SeaWorld.

You can take the **BaySide Skyride** above the bay or go up the **Skytower** for a great view of the bay as well as downtown. They're famous SeaWorld attractions.

Do you like roller coasters? Then you are in luck at SeaWorld San Diego. Manta is a steel coaster where you lay facedown underneath a giant manta ray. There are rolls, drops, and plenty of thrills for those at least 54 inches tall.

There's also Journey to Atlantis featuring a 60-foot waterfall plunge and Shipwreck Rapids to carry you through rapids and waterfalls (check out the sunbathing sea turtles!). Or journey to the Wild Arctic aboard a simulated jet. At the end, you meet beluga whales, polar bears, and other creatures of the frozen North.

Stop in at SeaWorld's Pole to Pole. There are hands-on activities as well as plenty of cuddly creatures and other souvenirs.

If you could take home an animal which one would it be?

DID YOU KNOW?

Penguins are birds, but they can't fly. Instead they swim through the sea at amazing speeds using their flippers as "wings." You can see more than 350 penguins at SeaWorld's Penguin Encounter, which is also home to one of the world's only successful emperor penguin breeding colonies outside the Antarctic.

Helping Sick Animals

An *endangered species* is an animal or plant in danger of disappearing completely from our planet. Many species are *threatened*, which means unless conservation efforts are started, they're likely to become endangered.

Sea turtles, sea otters, and manatees are some of the animals rescued by SeaWorld San Antonio, San Diego, and Orlando. It's been nearly 50 years since SeaWorld's rescue programs started and more than 23,000 animals have been rescued—more than 6,500 animals in California and nearly 500 just in one year.

They even support an Oiled Wildlife Care Center for animals who fall victim to oil spills (vetmed.ucdavis.edu/owcn).

Seals and sea lions are the most common to be rescued, especially young sea lions who have gotten stranded on the beaches. Marine mammals get stranded because they are sick, injured, or get separated from their mothers. They may get entangled in nets or accidentally ingest plastic. People report strandings by calling 800-541-SEAL. SeaWorld has a hospital complete with a place to do surgery, take X-rays, prepare food, and allow the animals to recover in special pools. You can visit SeaWorld's Rescue Plaza near Shamu Stadium to learn more.

Once the animals are healthy, whenever possible they are returned to the wild. If government officials say they can't be released, they remain at SeaWorld or are cared for at another facility.

Learn the Lingo!

bow—a leap out of the water by an animal, such as a dolphin, penguin, or sea lion.

breach—when a whale, dolphin, or sea lion jumps out of the water and lands on its side or back.

flukes—the horizontal lobes of the tail of a whale, dolphin, or porpoise, made of connective tissue (not bone).

lobtail—when the animals slap their tail flukes on the surface of the water.

spyhop—to rise vertically out of the water so that the eye is above the surface.

A LOCAL KID SAYS:
"My favorite thing to do at the beach is fly kites with my dad."
—Joe, 10

What's Cool? In-line skating or skateboarding along the 3-mile pedestrian boardwalk that runs along the sand at Pacific and Mission Beaches.

Not Just Any Park

Mission Bay is a huge water playground—the largest in the world—with places where you can sail, fish, swim, water-ski, and of course—surf.

On your visit, build sand castles, kayak, or watch the surfers and windsurfers. You can also go fishing or for a ride in a powerboat.

Like to bike, in-line skate, skateboard, or just race your brother or sister? There are 20 miles of paths right near the sand at the end of **Mission Beach** that run all the way north to Pacific Beach (2688 E. Mission Bay Dr.; 858-581-7602; sandiego.gov).

A lot of kids like to go to **Tecolote Shores.** It's a big park where you can fly kites, play Frisbee, or have a picnic.

If you like birds, head to **Fiesta Island** (directly south of the Hilton Hotel in East Mission Bay; 619-235-1169; sandiego.gov).

Nearby in **Belmont Park,** find the Giant Dipper coaster—it's got 13 hills! There's also bumper cars, a video arcade, a rock wall, and a FlowRider (3146 Mission Blvd.; 858-228-9283; belmontpark.com).

Ready to build a giant sand castle? Make sure you have a pail and shovel!

TELL THE ADULTS

Military personnel and their families can receive special discounts at SeaWorld (wavesofhonor.com). There are many discounted deals for admission to SeaWorld and other major San Diego attractions, such as the San Diego Zoo (seaworldparks .com/seaworld-sandiego/book-online/tickets/ mostpopulartourist).

You will find special fun events at SeaWorld throughout the year:

Summer Nights means extended park hours, fireworks, and nighttime animal shows and dance parties on the weekends.

On Saturday and Sunday in the month leading up to Halloween, there is SeaWorld's Halloween Spooktacular with sea-inspired trick or treat stations for kids in costume, a special Clyde and Seamore's Spooky Adventure sea lion and otter show, and *Sesame Street*'s Countdown to Halloween.

SeaWorld's Christmas Celebration starts before Thanksgiving with holiday-themed shows featuring Shamu, live reindeer, and more than a million holiday lights.

There are also plenty of opportunities to get close to your favorite animals when you plan in advance (check seaworldsadiego .com). Talk to the animal keepers and learn how they are trained. You can:

Dine with Shamu.

Interact with a beluga whale or a dolphin— you get in a wet suit and touch, feed, and give training signals to beluga whales. (Kids have to be at least 10 years old and 48 inches tall.)

Reach out and touch a dolphin during the Dolphin Encounter.

Have a personal Penguin Encounter.

Take a behind-the-scenes tour of SeaWorld and meet endangered sea turtles, penguins, or sharks.

Take part in a Sleepover at SeaWorld.

Aquatica

Waterslide or lazy river?

You'll find both those options and more at **Aquatica San Diego** (2052 Entertainment Circle, Chula Vista; 619-661-7373; aquaticabyseaworld.com).

Just make sure you stay safe! Set up a place where you know you can meet your parents. Observe all of the height requirements; some rides require or recommend life vests, especially if you are 42 inches and under.

Aquatica combines up-close animal encounters (think flamingos and turtles), thrills (check out the new Taumata Racer high-speed racing waterslide), and the chance to kick back on an inner tube (Loggerhead Lane's 1,250-foot lazy river). There are dozens of rides and attractions, including Big Surf Shores, one of the largest wave pools in Southern California, and an entire area for the youngest parkgoers, Kata's Kookaburra Cove.

Don't miss Walkabout Waters. The 4-story play area has slides, hoses, jets, geysers, and more water features. Every 5 minutes a 500-gallon bucket unloads water on everyone below!

DID YOU KNOW?

SeaWorld just launched generationnature.com to teach kids about conservation and protecting the environment.

KNOW YOUR SEA ANIMALS

Match these sea animals to their traits.

____ beluga whale   ____ green sea turtle

____ manatee   ____ manta ray

____ Asian small-clawed otter

A) This animal is closely related to sharks. It has a skeleton made out of cartilage instead of bone. It also loves to swim along the bottom of the ocean, sucking up its food from the mud. It can crush the hard shells of shellfish with its rows of flat teeth.

B) This animal is endangered. It is a reptile and can stay underwater for up to 5 hours. Some swim 1,300 miles during their migration, but they still return to the same beach every year to lay their eggs.

C) This animal is a mammal that looks like it is always smiling. It swims around under the very thick ice of the Arctic and is colored white so that it can camouflage into its surroundings.

D) This animal is an endangered marine mammal. Many of these are hurt each year by boat strikes. It loves to eat plants and can eat up to 200 pounds of food a day!

E) This animal lives in the fresh and brackish waters of Southeast Asia. It only weighs 2 to 11 pounds, and is very cute. It uses scent as its main form of communication with the others of its species.

See page 153 for the answers.

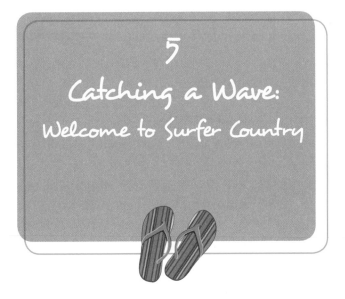

5

Catching a Wave:
Welcome to Surfer Country

Ready to catch the Big One?

You'll be in good company. San Diego is famous **surfer country.**

You'll see surfers of all ages in the ocean all year round, riding the waves. They're fun to watch—and to join, once you've had a lesson or two.

San Diego has 70 miles of coastline and many awesome spots to surf, paddleboard, kayak, and try your hand at any and every water sport. Take your pick of 33 public beaches!

San Onofre State Beach, at the northern tip of San Diego County, is the name for the 3 miles of beach here, and you'll have plenty of easy waves to play in (3030 Avenida Del Presidente, San Clemente; 949-492-4872; parks.ca.gov).

DID YOU KNOW?

Coronado Beach is considered one of the best beaches in the country (1800 Avenida de las Arenas, Coronado; sandiego.org).

Swami Beach is one of San Diego County's top surf spots, while those who want to try surfing for the first time head to the stretch along Pacific Beach and Mission Beach (1298 S. Coast Hwy. 101, Encinitas; 760-633-2740; beachcalifornia.com).

You have to take a staircase down to **Stone Steps Beach** in Encinitas, but you can stay up on the cliffs and watch the surfers from there too (336 Neptune Ave., Encinitas; ci.encinitas.ca.us).

Coronado—the island just across San Diego Bay from downtown—has the widest sand beach of any in San Diego County and pleases beginners as well as experienced surfers who head to North Beach.

{ **What's Cool?** Watching the surfers at Sunset Cliffs on the Point Loma Peninsula. The most daring come here!

You might even see how a surfboard gets made at the **TNT Surf Shop** in Imperial Beach. It's got a factory right there (206 Palm Ave., Imperial Beach; 619-424-8107; tnt surf.com).

Of course, there's plenty more to do on the beach besides surf: Build the biggest sand castle you've ever seen. Go boogie boarding. Watch people's pets splash around at dog-friendly spots like Dog Beach, at the end of North Beach in Coronado. Explore a tide pool at low tide. How many different creatures can you count?

Join your family at a bonfire on the beach at night.

A VISITING KID SAYS:
"Only bring shorts to San Diego because the weather is the best!"
—Adam, 13, New York, NY

Take a walk out on a pier like at Oceanside, about 45 minutes from downtown San Diego. You'll see a lot of anglers here. While you're at it, stop in at the **California Surf Museum** (312 Pier View Way, Oceanside; 760-721-6876; surfmuseum.org). Every summer, the World Body Surfing Championship is held here. Kids under 12 get in free!

Take in a concert. There are summer **Coronado Promenade Concerts** in Spreckels Park (121 Broadway, #600; 619-235-9500; coronadoconcert.com/concerts).

Don't forget shopping—whether you want to look like a surfer or just buy souvenirs. **Coronado's Ferry Landing** is a fun place to browse the shops—and to eat with its walkways, palm trees, and view of San Diego's skyline (1201 1st St., Coronado; 619-435-8895; coronadoferry landingshops.com).

Got your camera?

Point Loma

It's famous for its white-sand beaches, surfers, tide pools, and history. That's because the southern tip of Point Loma is where explorer Juan Rodriguez Cabrillo landed in San Diego Bay in 1542.

Today, the **Cabrillo National Monument** (1800 Cabrillo Memorial Dr.; 619-557-5450; nps.gov/cabr), which marks the site with his statue, is part of a 160-acre preserve. It's easy to see why it's one of the most visited national monuments in the country. In winter, the high cliffs are a great place to watch for whales, and the tide pools at the ocean edge are ideal for getting up close and personal to tiny sea creatures—starfish, crabs, anemones, and octopuses among them.

While you're there, check out the famous Old Point Loma Lighthouse too.

Remember to bring snacks or a picnic. There aren't restaurants at the monument.

DID YOU KNOW?

Exploring tide pools along the coast is best when the tide is the lowest. So check tide charts online before you visit!

Learning to Catch a Wave

There are lots of places in San Diego where kids can learn to surf:

- **Surf Diva** on La Jolla Shores (2160 Avenida de la Playa, La Jolla; 858-454-8273; surfdiva.com)

- **Ocean Experience** in Ocean Beach (4940 Newport Ave.; 619-225-0674; oceanexperience.net)

- **Pacific Surf School** in Mission Beach (669 Ocean Front Walk; 858-488-2685; pacificsurf.org)

- **San Diego Surfing Academy** (2530 Jefferson St., Carlsbad; 760-230-1474; surfsdsa.com)

A LOCAL KID SAYS:
"I tried surfing for the first time. It was really fun, but it's a lot harder than it looks!"
—Ellie, 11

Lifeguards

You'll see them winter and summer patrolling the miles and miles of coastline. They tell you where it's safe to swim and warn you if there are dangerous rip currents that will pull you out to sea. Most important, they'll come after you if you get in trouble.

It's a hard job. They watch the beaches and take care of the rescue equipment. They answer questions, make sure people are following the rules of the beach, administer first aid, and, of course, rescue those who need help. The good part is they get to spend every day at the beach!

To be a lifeguard, you've got to be in good shape to qualify and then pass a tough swimming test and physical exam. Then you must take a training course to learn everything from first aid to ocean rescues. You have to pass

A VISITING KID SAYS:
"I looked for crabs on the beach and collected them in a bucket."
—George, 10, Los Angeles, CA

a written test on all you've learned. Here are some things you can do to help lifeguards do their job—and keep yourself safe:

- Always swim in lifeguarded areas.

- Ask lifeguards about surf conditions before you go into the water and never dive into areas close to shore if you don't know how deep the water is.

- Always swim with a buddy or a grown-up.

- Don't panic if you get pulled by a rip current. Call for help. Try to swim at an angle toward shore.

- Avoid swimming near storm drain outlets.

DID YOU KNOW?

A Hawaiian named Duke Kahanamoku, an Olympic swimmer, is considered the father of surfing. He popularized the sport in California in the early 1920s. You can learn a lot about how surfgot started in California at California Surf Museum in Oceanside.

TELL THE ADULTS

Beaches and pools are lots of fun, but they can also be dangerous. The American Red Cross has developed a free Swim App that provides parents and kids with water safety tips as well as games. The vast majority of drownings occur when children are not being supervised (redcross.org/mobile-apps/swim-app).

Designate an adult to be a "water watcher." Take turns even if there's a lifeguard on duty. Adults should be "touching distance" to preschoolers and toddlers around the water. Don't rely on water wings or other inflatable toys either, pediatricians warn. They may give your child a false sense of security.

Insist that older kids swim with a buddy. Remind them to stay away from pool and hot tub drains where they can get sucked underwater.

{ **What's Cool?** Making a giant sand creation. Bring along an ice-cream scoop, spatula, ruler, butter knife, spray bottle, gardening trowel, pails, and shovels when you go to the beach. These items and some good ideas are all you need to build a sand sculpture. Here's a tip from the experts: Keep the sand really wet. And pack it really hard. Jump up and down on it. It works!

If visiting friends or relatives with a pool, make sure young children are carefully supervised at all times and that pool gates are locked.

Don't let kids swim unsupervised—even if there's a lifeguard on duty. Parents should watch younger kids every second around the pool or ocean.

Drowning is the leading cause of accidental death for young children in California.

When boating, even if you're great swimmers, always wear Coast Guard–approved life jackets.

DID YOU KNOW?

Many believe the famous historic **Hotel del Coronado** is haunted by a young woman named Kate Morgan, who checked in in 1892 and never checked out (1500 Orange Ave., Coronado; reservations, 800-468-3533, information, 619-435-6611; hoteldel.com).

WORD SEARCH: TALK LIKE A SURFER

When you surf, you ride on the forward face of a wave toward shore. It's harder than it looks! At least you can talk like a surfer. They have a language of their own.

A **gremmie** is a beginning surfer. He'd be **stoked** (very happy) to be on these beaches, but might end up **taking gas** (losing control). Surfers call really great waves **all time.** Here's some more surfer lingo:

Bail: To step off the board in order to avoid being knocked off.

Shoulder: The unbroken part of the wave.

Gnarly: What surfers call large, difficult waves.

Bomb: An exceptionally large wave.

Pop-Up: Going from lying on the board to standing—in one jump!

Quiver: A surfer's collection of boards.

DID YOU KNOW?

Many of the world's top surfers aged 20 and younger come here in the spring for the Oakley Pro Junior (oakleyprojunior.com). You can watch if you are in town.

CIRCLE THE SURFER TERMS!

all time	bail
bomb	gnarly
gremmie	pop-up
quiver	shoulder
stoked	taking gas

```
T  A  K  I  N  G  G  A  S  B  V  M  S
A  L  A  B  V  R  S  U  V  S  E  T  O
B  L  S  M  R  E  O  E  U  E  G  Q  A
E  T  R  O  B  M  A  R  P  O  P  U  P
R  I  E  C  T  M  A  B  N  A  H  I  R
U  M  A  N  L  I  E  R  R  R  T  V  F
B  E  T  Q  L  E  C  S  T  O  K  E  D
X  B  A  Z  B  O  N  H  M  N  S  R  S
M  R  R  Y  O  C  C  O  L  A  E  G  S
Q  N  I  O  R  A  H  U  M  L  T  R  B
Y  F  O  G  N  A  R  L  Y  N  C  W  O
J  U  S  M  S  O  C  D  N  A  L  G  M
E  C  V  Y  T  N  R  E  E  W  R  E  B
B  A  I  L  M  E  U  R  O  N  I  C  A
```

See page 153 for the answers.

6

La Jolla

(Sounds Like La Hoya): Hiking, Snorkeling & Whale Watching

Ready to take a hike?

You're in the right place in La Jolla at **Torrey Pines State Reserve.** It spans 2,000 acres and is named for the Torrey pine tree. It's really fun to hike when you can see the ocean from the trail (12600 N. Torrey Pines Rd., La Jolla; 858-755-2063; torreypine.org).

You'll also see birds, reptiles, butterflies, and all kinds of native plants. Check out the animal tracks! The kids corner on the park website can help you identify them.

A LOCAL KID SAYS:

"My favorite thing to do outside in San Diego is to hike to Potato Chip Rock on Mount Woodson."
—Chase, 14

DID YOU KNOW?

You might see dolphins or whales when you hike along the coast at Torrey Pines State Reserve in La Jolla.

Can you find the mountain lion track or the skunk?

Park naturalists say the best time to find tracks on the trails is early in the morning before many hikers have been by. The more people who have been on the trail ahead of you, the more likely it is that the tracks have been trampled. Some of the best places to find tracks are near water.

Stop in at the visitor center. Maybe you'll want to take a guided walk with a naturalist who can tell you all about the area. Watch the birds at **Los Penasquitos Lagoon.**

Of course, you're going to want to go to the beach in La Jolla too. La Jolla is a neighborhood within San Diego, but it will feel like a separate city with lots of beautiful houses, fancy stores, restaurants, and those amazing beaches.

DID YOU KNOW?

More than 70 percent of the earth's surface is covered by ocean.

You can see hundreds of seals just south of La Jolla Cove at the **Children's Pool. Seal Rock** just offshore is a protected reserve for them.

A lot of families like to go to **La Jolla Cove,** where they have lifeguards (1100 Coast Blvd., La Jolla; lajollabythesea .com/la-jolla-cove). Check out the sandstone cliffs!

You'd think the **Children's Pool** would be for kids, but sand has filled in much of the area inside the seawall so now it's a great place to see seals. They make a lot of noise!

Go to **La Jolla Shores** to kayak, play beach volleyball, or have a picnic. You'll like the long boardwalk!

Like caves? If you are brave, you can walk 145 steps down a tunnel to the largest of the **caves** in La Jolla Cove.

DID YOU KNOW?

An amazing diversity of fish and invertebrates make their home within underwater kelp forests, a crucial ocean ecosystem. You can see one of these habitats at the **Birch Aquarium** in La Jolla.

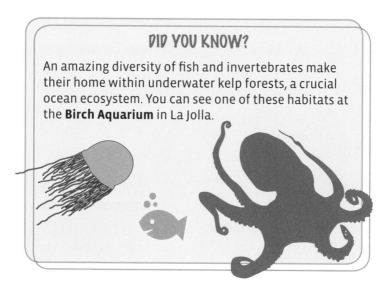

If you enjoy snorkeling, you'll love **La Jolla Underwater Park and Ecological Preserve.** This is the place to see all kinds of marine creatures up close in crystal clear water (off of La Jolla between Ellen Browning Scripps Park and La Jolla Shores; sandiegocoastlife.com).

Go to the **Gliderport** and watch the hang gliders and paragliders. Maybe your parents would let you try on a tandem with an instructor (2800 Torrey Pines Scenic Dr., La Jolla; 858-452-9858; flytorrey.com).

Hang gliding or tide pooling, snorkeling, kayaking, or hiking: The hardest part in La Jolla is choosing what to do—and getting everyone in your family to agree!

A VISITING KID SAYS:
"Kids should not leave California without trying In-N-Out burgers. In my opinion, they're the best!"
—Genesis, 12, Los Angeles, CA

What's in Your Backpack?

When you're going hiking or to the beach, kids say you need:

- A reusable water bottle filled with water—two if you are going on a long hike! Put stickers on it and it becomes a souvenir.

- A rain jacket

- Snacks. You can make your own trail mix!

- A phone to take pictures (and keep in touch in case you get separated from your parents)

- Band-Aids

- Sunscreen

A LOCAL KID SAYS:
"Kids who are visiting San Diego should get ready to have a lot of fun!"
—Edward, 10

Whale Watching

Look for the "blow." When a whale comes up to breathe, it sends a cloud of air and water up as high as 15 feet. Watch for blows 30–50 seconds apart.

Each winter, thousands of gray whales travel south from Alaska along California's coast to Baja, where they have their babies, and then farther south. The trip is 5,000 miles—the longest any mammal migrates each year.

You can see them in the winter from the San Diego coast because they travel in small groups fairly close to the shore.

It's easier to see them when you go out on a whale watching boat. There are many companies that offer these trips, including **Hornblower Cruises** that has experts from the San Diego Natural History Museum on board (970 N. Harbor Dr. at USS *Midway*; 888-467-6256; hornblower.com).

Flagship Cruises and Events has Birch Aquarium naturalists on board (990 N. Harbor Dr.; 619-234-4111; flagshipsd.com).

You'll get to see seabirds, seals, and dolphins! If you're lucky, they will jump out of the water and fall back in, making a huge splash.

Don't forget your binoculars!

Artist or Art Lover?

Both? You will be right at home exploring the **Museum of Contemporary Art** in La Jolla (700 Prospect St., La Jolla; 858-454-3541; mcasd.org). This is a good place to see works by California artists, but you'll also find pieces done by the famous artists from around the world.

Stop by the Thought Lab to share your ideas about the art you're seeing. Check out the ocean view from the Edwards Garden Gallery. There's the giant *Hammering Man* sculpture and the colorful *Big Ganeesh* painted with automotive paint.

Most important, see what you think of the contemporary art—there's painting, sculpture, photographs, and drawings. There are locations here and downtown. You might even see something created by a San Diego kid. What could you create?

DID YOU KNOW?
Kids get in free at the Museum of Contemporary Art in La Jolla.

84

Making Sea Friends

Watch as sharks cruise by eyeing their food or as lobsters emerge from their rocky hiding places.

At the **Birch Aquarium** in La Jolla—it's part of the Scripps Institution of Oceanography at UC San Diego (300 Kennel Way, La Jolla; 858-534-3474; aquarium.ucsd.edu)—you can see sea creatures get fed, explore a tide pool, or go snorkeling with a naturalist who can explain what is around you.

This is a great place to learn all about the creatures that live in the Pacific Ocean and how the environment—and what we do—impacts them. This is more than an aquarium, though. There are a lot of researchers who work here too.

You might meet some of them during **SEA Days,** which offer special hands-on activities. Spot leopard sharks, garibaldi, eels, barracuda, giant sea bass, and more in the 2-story, 70,000-gallon tank that houses the **Kelp Forest.** There's even a high-definition Kelp Cam!

Find out about all kinds of Pacific marine life at the **Arthur M. and Kate F. Tode Hall of Fishes,** from the cold waters of the Pacific Northwest along the California coast to the tropical waters of Mexico and the Caribbean.

Make sure to say hi to the giant Pacific octopus!

TELL THE ADULTS

Whenever you are hiking with kids:

Make sure you have a plan in place in case some-one gets separated from the group. Tell the kids to "hug a tree" and stay where they are until you return for them. Make sure they have your cell phone number and where you are staying written on a card in their pocket. They may not remember!

Have reusable water bottles and healthy snacks in everyone's backpack.

Use sunscreen, even if it is cloudy.

Stash rain gear in the packs.

Remember it is about the journey! If everyone gets tired or the hike is too difficult, just turn back.

{ **What's Cool?** The Preuss Tide Pool Plaza overlooking the Pacific Ocean at the Birch Aquarium with three living tide pools for hands-on fun.

USE THE SPACE BELOW TO DRAW PICTURES OF WHAT YOU SAW TODAY!

7

LEGOLAND:
Driving School, Pirates &
Mini Lego Cities

Ready to make something

happen? Not only will you see all kinds of fun things at **LEGOLAND** California, but you can make things happen at each of the rides and attractions (1 Legoland Dr., Carlsbad; 760-918-5346; california.legoland.com).

Explore hidden tombs and hunt for treasure in the **Land of Adventure.**

If you have younger brothers and sisters or cousins with you, you'll have fun at the **Explore Village** made with tons of DUPLO bricks. Check out the life-size giraffes, zebras, and lions or drench your parents standing below the Rain Maker. They'll also like **Dino Island** where kids can lie down inside a life-sized dino footprint or become a resident of **DUPLO Playtown.** Check out the fire station!

A VISITING KID SAYS:
"You're never too old for LEGOLAND because they are adding a bunch of stuff all the time that makes it fun."
—Sean, 13, Orange County, CA

Go to Driving School in **Fun Town** or cycle your way up on people-powered pedal cars. You can walk through a mini-factory making LEGOS.

Ready to get wet? At **Pirate Shores** you fire water cannons across the ships' bows, sail through a skull at **Splash Battle,** or barrel down **Treasure Falls,** plunging nearly 12 feet.

Create your own hero (or villain) at the **LEGO Hero Factory** at the Imagination Zone. Race a life-size **LEGO TECHNIC** along a roller coaster or build and test your own LEGO car—and race it against your brother's or your dad's! The more you spin on the **BIONICLE Blaster,** the faster you'll go.

A VISITING KID SAYS:
"If you bring LEGO mini figures to LEGOLAND, you can exchange them and you can build your own LEGO character to take home."
—Alexander, 7, Phoenix, AZ

There are 60 interactive attractions here, as well as a water park and **SEA LIFE Aquarium.** (Tell your parents you can get a combined ticket!) Did you know there are only two LEGOLANDS in the US—here in California and in Winterhaven, Florida, near Orlando.

Check out the **minigolf** at Wild Woods Golf—complete with LEGO sculptures of woodland creatures, and take a thrill ride at Castle Hill where you can choose how intense you want your robo-coaster ride at the Knights' Tournament. Try out **Granny's Apple Fries** while you're there! You can pan for gold at the King's Treasury or hit The Hideaways, an adventure playground complete with ropes, cargo nets, and slides.

Everyone loves **Miniland USA** because you notice something different every time you visit:

- The most famous scenes from the *Star Wars* movies at the LEGO Star Wars Gallery.

- The tiny wedding chapel in Las Vegas and the famous Las Vegas strip.

A VISITING KID SAYS:
"I like how there is a playground inside the LEGOLAND Hotel with lots of LEGOS to play with."
—Luke, 11, Orange County, CA

- Push the buttons at the New England countryside and watch the LEGO people and animals come to life.

- The animated marching band saluting the new president in the Washington, DC, area where tiny LEGO cherry blossoms bloom in the spring.

- Floats parading during Mardi Gras in New Orleans.

- The yellow taxicabs driving the streets of Times Square in New York.

- The California Coastline complete with San Diego surfers.

Now that you've seen all these giant and tiny LEGO creations, go to the Model Shop and watch the Master Model Builders create new LEGO models for the park.

A LOCAL KID SAYS:
"My favorite at LEGOLAND is the TECHNIC Coaster."
—Vincent, 8

Time to create your own mini-me LEGO person to take home!

Flower Power

Have you ever spelled your name in plants?

You can at the special Spell and Smell Garden that's part of the Hamilton Children's Garden at the **San Diego Botanic Garden** in Encinitas (230 Quail Gardens Dr., Encinitas, CA; 760-436-3036; sdbgarden.org).

The Botanic Garden is huge, with more than 4,000 plants on display. But you'll probably want to spend your time at the Children's Garden. You can help water the vegetables and fruits that are growing in the Incredible Edible Garden, learning what's in season. Check out the worm composting bin, and pot a succulent plant to take home.

You can also pot a plant in the sand and use big wood blocks to build a balsa fort in the Earth Builder area, or paint pictures with chalk on a giant board in the Art Garden.

There's even a Music Garden, where you can try out instruments, and a maze to wander through. What can you build with the huge foam blocks, ramps, and balls at the Tropical Surround? That's if you want to leave Toni's Tree House (30 Quail Gardens Dr., Encinitas, CA; 760-436-3036; sdbgarden.org).

Come to San Diego in spring and you can run through 50 acres blooming with flowers of all colors down a hillside at the Flower Fields at Carlsbad Ranch. The flowers bloom for about six to eight weeks, from early March through early May (5704 Paseo Del Norte, Carlsbad, CA; 860-431-0352; theflowerfields .com).

What's your favorite color flower?

Adventurer or Royalty?

You choose what kind of room you want and you'll find LEGO models and decor to match at the **LEGOLAND Hotel** at the entrance to LEGOLAND. Check out the treasure chest in the room. But you've got to complete a treasure hunt in your room first (1 Legoland Dr., Carlsbad; 760-918-5346; california.legoland.com/legoland-hotel)!

When you stay here, you can hit the park early before it gets too crowded.

Look around—there are 3,433 LEGO models in the hotel including a family of dragons, one of which is a giant dragon that breathes smoke at the entrance, and there is another that blows bubbles in the bathtub on the patio.

There's a huge Castle Play area complete with pirate ship and interactive castle, a restaurant with a kid-size buffet, and a disco elevator. As you enter, lights flash in the ceiling, music plays, and a mirrored ball spins.

You'll be having so much fun you won't want to go to sleep!

{ **What's Cool?** The Build-A-Raft River at LEGOLAND Water Park. You customize your own raft made from soft LEGO bricks before you float down a lazy river.

Just Add Water

LEGOLAND Water Park has a wave pool, Build-A-Raft lazy river, tube slides, body slides, and a huge interactive water-play structure (1 Legoland Dr., Carlsbad; 760-918-5346; california.legoland.com).

There's plenty for littler kids too, at the DUPLO splash area with DUPLO creatures everywhere.

Check out the Twin Chasers—you ride down side by side in enclosed red tube slides—nearly 130 feet. The Splash Out slide takes you down 240 feet where you splash out into the water. Four of you can ride together on Orange Rush—it's even longer!

Make sure to check out the Imagination Station where you can build bridges, dams, and cities out of DUPLO bricks and test them against the water flow. There's even a musical water stand that lets you conduct a water symphony as you cover holes, creating musical notes.

Joker Soaker has all kinds of slides—watch out for the huge bucket that dumps on you!

DID YOU KNOW?

The trash cans, recycling bins, and benches throughout the LEGOLAND Water Park are made of recycled milk jugs.

TELL THE ADULTS

- You should all get out of the sun every 90 minutes or so for a short break. Make sure to get plenty to drink so you don't get dehydrated. Wear a hat and sunglasses with UV protection.

- What you need: sunscreen that is considered "broad spectrum" and that has a sun protection factor, or SPF, of 15 and above. Broad spectrum is FDA's new way to describe a sunscreen that blocks both types of damaging rays.

- Re-apply every two hours, according to the American Academy of Pediatrics, even on cloudy days and especially after the kids have been in the water.

- Keep infants out of the sun as much as possible. Dress infants in lightweight long pants, long-sleeved shirts, and brimmed hats that shade the neck to prevent sunburn. However, when adequate clothing and shade are not available, parents can apply a minimal amount of sunscreen with at least SPF 15 to small areas, the American Academy of Pediatrics recommends. If an infant gets sunburn, apply cold compresses to the affected area.

FILL IN THE MISSING LETTERS IN THE NAMES OF THE FUN PLACES YOU CAN VISIT AT LEGOLAND!

1) C____stle Hil____

2) Din____ Islan____

3) ____UPLO Vill____ge

4) F____n To____n

4) Ima____ination ____one

6) ____and of Adven____ure

7) Min____land U____A

8) Pir____te Shore____

See page 154 for the answers.

DID YOU KNOW?

There are more than 22,000 LEGO models in LEGOLAND created from more than 52 million LEGO bricks—from a tiny rabbit in a magician's hat to a giant brontosaurus. What's your favorite?

8

Fish Tacos,
Cuddly Creatures &
Pro Ball

Ever eaten a fish taco?

San Diego is famous for them. They're usually made with fried fish topped with a mayonnaise sauce, shredded cabbage, lime, and salsa. That's probably very different from the meat or chicken tacos you're used to.

One of the best parts of vacation is trying new things—whether it's food, a sport you've never attempted, or a huge roller coaster at a theme park.

A VISITING KID SAYS:
"Don't leave without trying Mexican food. You can get yummy Mexican food in Old Town."
—Katarina, 8, Long Beach Island, NJ

Isn't it fun to challenge yourself? San Diego is a great place to taste new foods, especially fish, because it is located on the Pacific Coast near Mexico—just 15 miles from downtown—and fish is used in many Mexican dishes. Make it a goal to try something you've never eaten before—like a fish taco or fresh tamale.

Of course, you'll find plenty of pizza, burgers, and places for ice cream and cupcakes for dessert. Local kids like **Babycakes** in Balboa Park (2221 Morley Field Dr.; 619-220-4990; babycakessandiego.com).

But there are also plenty of spots offering food from all around the world. Ask the people who work at the hotel where you're staying where their kids like to go out to eat.

DID YOU KNOW?

Many San Diego restaurants offer some version of the fish taco because everyone loves them so much.

{ **What's Cool?** Lunch from one of San Diego's food trucks. There's even a Sweet Treats Truck (sdfoodtrucks.com)!

San Diego is also a great place to shop for things you might not find at home. Besides the special souvenirs you can get at SeaWorld, LEGOLAND, and the San Diego Zoo, you'll find good shopping in:

- **Seaport Village** (849 W. Harbor Dr.; 619-235-4014; seaportvillage.com) along San Diego's waterfront with more than 50 stores, including **Apple Box Toys** where you can get a personalized wooden toy or sign for your room (837 W. Harbor Dr.; 800-676-7529; appleboxtoys .com) and **Kite Flite** (849 W. Harbor Dr.; 619-234-5483; kiteflitesd.com).

A VISITING KID SAYS:
"Kids should get something from the USS *Midway* Museum like a model jet or a helicopter."
—William, 10, Phoenix, AZ

- **Old Town** (4002 Wallace St.; 619-220-5422; oldtown sandiego.org) with souvenirs from Mexico. Head to the **Old Town Market** (4010 Twiggs St.; 619-278-0955; oldtownmarketssandiego.com) where there are lots of carts with things from Mexico and South America whether you want a Day of the Dead doll or a souvenir for your pet.

- **Westfield Horton Plaza** that covers 6 blocks in the Gaslamp Quarter (324 Horton Plaza; 619-238-1596; westfield.com/hortonplaza).

- **Mission Bay** (3448 Crown Point Dr.; sandiego.org) where there are plenty of souvenir shops along the boardwalk for T-shirts, and along Mission Boulevard to buy surfer and skate clothes. If you're looking for that perfect shell, stop in at **Ocean Gifts & Shells** (4934 Newport Ave., Mission Bay; 619-980-2651; oceangifts andshells.com).

What are you taking home with you?

DID YOU KNOW?

California has a larger population than the entire country of Canada. It has one-third more people than Texas, the next biggest state. Many are immigrants who have come from other countries to settle here.

Play Ball!

Of course games are rarely called for rain nor will you freeze watching football. You can join local kids and their parents:

- Cheering on the **San Diego Padres** at Petco Park in the heart of downtown (100 Park Blvd.; 619-795-5000; sandiego.padres.mlb.com)

A LOCAL KID SAYS:
"I like watching the Padres play from the sandbox in the outfield."
—Hector, 11

- Watching the **San Diego Chargers** at Qualcomm Stadium (9449 Friars Rd., Mission Valley; 858-874-4500; chargers.com)

- Joining college football fans at the **Holiday Bowl** at the end of December at Qualcomm Stadium (9449 Friars Rd., Mission Valley; 619-283-5808; holidaybowl.com)

- Seeing male and female college athletes compete in your favorite sport like basketball, volleyball, tennis, and soccer at:
  - **San Diego State University** (5500 Campanile Dr.; 619-594-5200; goaztecs.cstv.com)
  - The **University of California at San Diego** (9500 Gilman Dr., La Jolla; 858-534-2230; ucsdtritons.com)
  - The **University of San Diego** (5998 Alcalá Park; 619-260-4600; usdtoreros.cstv.com)

Souvenirs

Are you a stuffed koala, Shamu, or personalized LEGO person? Maybe you'd rather have something to wear or put on your backpack that reminds you of the baseball or football game you saw or simply says SAN DIEGO.

A VISITING KID SAYS:
"You shouldn't leave San Diego without a seashell from the beach."
—Chloe, 9, Scottsdale, AZ

I ♥ SAN DIEGO

DID YOU KNOW?

The museums in Balboa Park have great gift shops, especially at the **Reuben H. Fleet Science Center** (1875 El Prado, Balboa Park; 619-238-1233; rhfleet.org).

Good Eats

Bo-Beau Kitchen and Garden in La Mesa (8384 La Mesa Blvd., La Mesa; 619-337-3445; cohnrestaurants.com) has a big school bus for kids to play on. There is also a great chef for Mom and Dad, as well as a kids' menu that features grilled sea bass, roast chicken, and mini steak frites. Classics include mac and cheese and pasta. Eat outside in the garden!

Corvette Diner (2965 Historic Decatur Rd.; 619-542-1476; cohnrestaurants.com) offers music and car-themed rooms, an arcade, and a kid-friendly menu. The waitstaff, dressed in 1950s-era outfits, tosses straws and bubble gum on the tables. Try the sliders!

Fiesta de Reyes (2754 Calhoun St.; 619-297-3100; fiestade reyes.com) in the heart of Old Town San Diego State Historic Park boasts shopping, two Mexican restaurants, and mariachi singers. The restaurants at Fiesta de Reyes—Casa de Reyes and Barra Barra Saloon—are known for serving some of the best Mexican food and margaritas in San Diego.

In-N-Out Burger (in-n-outburger.com) has more than 200 locations in Southern California, including in and around San Diego. It's fast food with a difference. The burgers are made from meat free of additives, fillers, and preservatives. The fries come from potatoes straight from the farm, and the shakes are put together with real ice cream.

Lefty's Chicago Pizzeria (3448 30th St.; 619-295-1720; and 4030 Goldfinch St.; 619-299-4030; leftyspizza.com) has owners who promise authentic Chicago-style deep dish and stuffed pizzas.

Stone Brewing World Bistro & Gardens (1999 Citracado Pkwy., Escondido; 760-471-4999; and 2816 Historic Decatur Rd.; 619-269-2100; stoneworldbistro.com) has a big grassy lawn where kids can wander safely. There are two locations of this brewpub where the kids' menu offers up chicken stir-fry with noodles and a chicken and cheese burrito. Of course, there are plenty of local brews for Mom and Dad to try!

The Wave House (3146 Mission Blvd.; 858-228-9283; wave house.com) on the Mission Beach Boardwalk comes complete with tropical palms, a beanbag toss, and giant chessboard. The real attraction: watching beginning and expert surfers on the FlowRider wave simulators. Kids like quesadillas and chicken satay, but there are plenty of choices for parents—and spectacular ocean views.

TELL THE ADULTS

Farmers' markets are great places to teach kids where their food comes from. They can talk to farmers, see different vegetables and fruits they might not have at home, and gather fresh supplies for a picnic! You'll also find gourmet food, arts and crafts, and more. Farmers' markets are certified by the county agricultural commissioner, ensuring that the produce is being sold by the grower, is grown in California, and meets all California quality standards.

You can visit a farmers' market in San Diego any time of year any day of the week (sdfarmbureau.org has a full list). Bring cash and a bag to stow your purchases. Here are four popular choices:

The Hillcrest Farmers Market held every Sunday. Try the fresh tamales! There are 29 produce vendors selling fresh seasonal produce and dozens of artisans (University Avenue and Normal Street, all the way north to Lincoln; hillcrestfamersmarket.com).

DID YOU KNOW?

More than half of California kids and their parents don't speak English at home. They speak Spanish, Chinese, Korean, Vietnamese, and many other languages—some 200 languages are spoken in California.

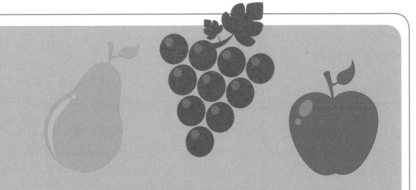

Coronado Farmers Market sets up along the bay on Tuesday, and besides fresh produce you'll find organic cheese here. It's right at the Coronado Ferry Landing (1st and B Streets, Coronado; sdfarm bureau.org).

Little Italy Mercato on Saturday is the place to buy gifts like cheese, olive oil, and pasta. Get a sandwich and Italian pastry to take to the beach. You've got 150 vendors to choose from (Date Street between India and Columbia Streets; littleitalymercato.com). And there is live music while you shop!

Ocean Beach Farmers Market on Wednesday afternoons features tidbits from local restaurants, music, and samples of local fruit. It attracts a lot of shoppers from outside the immediate area (4900 block of Newport Avenue between Cable and Bacon Streets in Ocean Beach; oceanbeachsandiego.com).

Eating Smart on Vacation

Vacations are a good time to try different foods other than just what is on a kids' menu. That's especially true in San Diego where you'll find every variety of food and plenty that is grown locally. Here's how you can eat healthier and try new foods:

- Split a portion of something with your brother or sister, or your mom or dad.

- If there is something you like on the grown-up menu, ask if you can get a half portion or order an appetizer size.

- Opt for fruit as a snack instead of chips or candy.

- Visit and talk to the farmers at the farmers' markets.

- Drink water rather than a soda. Your reusable bottle becomes a souvenir when you put stickers on it from all the places in San Diego you've been!

A LOCAL KID SAYS:
"No one can leave San Diego without trying some REAL Mexican food."
—Dex, 12

WHAT ARE THE PARTS OF A PLANT THAT WE EAT?

There are six plant parts that we eat: roots, stems, leaves, flowers, fruits, and seeds.

Draw a line between each vegetable and its type.

Root	Lettuce
Stem	Tomato
Leaves	Sunflower Seeds
Flower	Asparagus
Fruit	Broccoli
Seed	Carrot

What are the four things that all plants need to survive?

1) _____

2) _____

3) _____

4) _____

See page 154 for the answers.

9

Disneyland:
Mickey Mouse, Buzz Lightyear & Princess Power

It all started because Walt

Disney got tired of taking his kids to the merry-go-round. *There ought to be someplace better where parents and kids could have fun together,* he kept thinking.

That "someplace" became **Disneyland** (1313 Disneyland Railroad, Anaheim; 714-781-4565; disneyland.disney.go .com). After years of planning and dreaming, he opened the park in 1955 with just 18 attractions (the big pirate ship in Fantasyland was only half painted on opening day!). Disney had sunk all his money in the project. Few expected it to last.

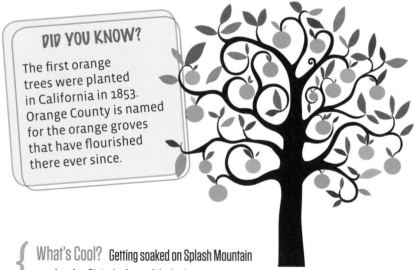

DID YOU KNOW?

The first orange trees were planted in California in 1853. Orange County is named for the orange groves that have flourished there ever since.

{ **What's Cool?** Getting soaked on Splash Mountain on a hot day. Sit in the front of the log!

Boy were they wrong! More than a half century later, Disneyland has entertained kings, athletes, astronauts, and celebrities from all over the world as well as tens of millions of parents and kids and was the inspiration for Walt Disney World in Florida and Disney Parks around the world.

Today there are some 60 major attractions spread out in 8 theme "lands" across 85 acres: Main Street, USA; Adventureland; Critter Country; Frontierland; Fantasyland; Tomorrowland; New Orleans Square; and Mickey's Toontown.

Next door is **Disney California Adventure** (1313 S. Disneyland Dr., Anaheim; 714-781-4565; disneyland.disney .go.com/disneys-california-adventure), a theme park all about California, which we'll get into in the next chapter.

A VISITING KID SAYS:
"If you time it right, you can be on the Matterhorn when the fireworks are going off."
—Bailee, 13, Flagstaff, AZ

Whatever land you visit, you'll find some thrills, some laughs, and plenty of fun. The ghosts seem real at the **Haunted Mansion;** so do the animals—alligators among them—on the **Jungle Cruise** (check out those headhunters!).

Enter **Fantasyland** through Sleeping Beauty's Castle, where you can climb into bobsleds for a twisting ride through the Matterhorn's ice caverns—right into an alpine lake. Watch out for the Abominable Snowman. Younger kids like to take **Peter Pan's Flight to Never, Never Land.** You'll meet Dumbo the Flying Elephant, Pinocchio, Snow White, and other characters from Disney animated films here. Nearby is a ride everyone will love: **It's a Small World.** A small boat takes you around the world, as you are serenaded by hundreds of mechanized children and animals dressed in native costumes from dozens of countries.

A VISITING KID SAYS:
"I did Space Mountain twice. I like that it is dark and you don't know where you are going!"
—Adam, 11, El Paso, TX

If you like thrills, you'll love **Splash Mountain** in Critter Country where you race down the mountain in a log flume—dropping 5 stories into a pond as more than 100 characters like Brer Rabbit entertain you.

In New Orleans Square, you can head out on a voyage with the **Pirates of the Caribbean** and sail directly into battle. Visit the port as it's overtaken by drunken pirates—some of whom land in jail.

The cartoon stars moved to **Mickey's Toontown,** the story goes, to get away from Hollywood. Stop in and see Mickey Mouse at his house (Pluto's dog-house is in the garden). You'll find Mickey in his Movie Barn. Here's your chance to get his autograph or take a picture with him. Minnie lives next door in a pink and purple house. Minnie will pose for pictures, too.

A LOCAL KID SAYS:
"My favorite attraction at Disneyland is the Star Tours. It's 3-D and inspired by Star Wars."
—Justin, 13

{ What's Cool? The coasters at Magic Mountain. There are more big ones than at just about any other park.

Roller-coaster fans won't be able to get enough of **Space Mountain** in Tomorrowland. It took more than a million hours to design and build the ride that blasts off and hurtles you through space—all in the dark. You also won't want to miss **Buzz Lightyear Astro Blasters.**

Another great roller coaster is **Big Thunder Mountain Railroad** in Frontierland, where you'll rock and roll through an underground earthquake. Take a break on **Tom Sawyer Island** in Frontierland and then figure out where to go next.

{ **What's Cool?** Mickey Mouse ears with your name on them. You can get them at the Mad Hatter in Fantasyland and on Main Street and the Gag Factory in Toontown, Tomorrowland, and elsewhere.

Who Was Walt Disney?

When Walt was a kid, he thought the clouds looked like animals. He grew up to be a talented cartoonist, and in 1928—more than 80 years ago—he created a cartoon mouse. His first movie was a black-and-white cartoon (no color in those days) called *Steamboat Willie,* and it was a huge success. He went on to make other famous animated movies. But Walt Disney had a problem. He'd take his daughters to amusement parks but couldn't find enough rides where he could have fun, too. So he decided to build a park where grown-ups could have fun along with kids. Disneyland opened in Anaheim in 1955 and was an immediate success. So many families loved it, he decided to build an even bigger park—Disney World in Orlando, Florida. He died before Disney World opened in 1971, but his brother Roy and all of the very talented people who worked for him made sure the Florida park was the way he would have wanted.

DID YOU KNOW?

Mickey Mouse was almost named Mortimer. Walt Disney's wife Lillian convinced him to go with Mickey instead.

Main Street, USA, is partly based on Marceline, Missouri, where Walt Disney grew up.

FASTPASS

Want to skip the lines? So does everyone. That's why Disney created the FASTPASS for its most popular attractions. Here's how it works. You go to the FAST-PASS machine at the entrances to the attractions and put in your park ticket. You'll get another ticket with the time you should return when you can pretty much walk right in. While you're waiting, you can head to other attractions that don't have long

lines, like Disneyland's Railroad, It's a Small World, or Tom Sawyer Island. Eat or shop while you're waiting instead of standing in a line. Just remember you can't get another FASTPASS for another attraction for a few hours (read the fine print on your ticket!). And make sure you get the FASTPASS for the attractions you most want to see early in the day because the numbers are limited and they will run out on busy days. You can see all the FASTPASS attractions on your map. Soon, you may be able to arrange to get a FASTPASS before you even arrive at the park. Disney has just introduced new MyMagic+ technology in Orlando that enables you to preload your FASTPASS at home for certain times. It is expected to be introduced in California.

Autographs & Photos

Keep that autograph book handy! There are plenty of places to meet up with the characters at the parks, but sometimes you'll have to wait in line for the opportunity. And sometimes, you get there just as the characters are leaving! Some of the best spots are Toontown (Mickey, Minnie, Donald, Goofy, Pooh and Pals) and Fantasyland's Castle Fantasy Faire.

If you want to meet Mickey, go to his Toontown house—as soon as it opens!

Tell your parents to check that day's guide map to see where your favorite characters will be. Another way to guarantee that you can meet and greet your favorites is to have your parents book a character meal. The characters come around to your table while you are eating to pose for pictures and sign autographs. Which characters do you most want to meet?

A LOCAL KID SAYS:
"I always carry around a camera for pictures and money for souvenirs at a theme park."
—Guadalupe, 15

Camp Snoopy & Monster Coasters

There are two other theme parks nearby that are popular with parents and kids—**Six Flags Magic Mountain** (26101 Magic Mountain Pkwy., Valencia; 661-255-4100; sixflags.com/magicmountain) and **Knott's Berry Farm** (8039 Beach Blvd., Buena Park; 714-220-5200; knotts.com). Adjacent to Knott's Berry Farm is a separate water park, too—**Soak City Orange County** (8039 Beach Blvd., Buena Park; 714-220-5200; soakcityoc.com).

Knott's Berry Farm is divided into areas representing different times in California history, from Ghost Town to Indian Trails, showcasing Native American crafts and culture. Fiesta Village highlights California's Spanish heritage. The Boardwalk celebrates Southern California beach towns, and Camp Snoopy focuses on California's High Sierra. Younger kids especially like Camp Snoopy with more than 30 kid-size attractions. At Halloween, when Knott's Berry Farm is known for its very scary Halloween Haunt, there's also a Snoopy's Costume Party for younger kids.

If you like roller coasters, you'll love Boomerang. You're turned upside down six times in less than a minute. If that's not enough of a thrill, try Montezooma's Revenge, where you zip through a 76-foot loop frontward—and backward.

Six Flags Magic Mountain is about an hour and a half from Anaheim and famous for roller coasters. It is best for kids over 42 inches tall, though there are some shows and rides for younger kids, including the **Hurricane Harbor** water park next door (26101 Magic Mountain Pkwy., Valencia; 661-255-4527; sixflags.com/hurricaneharborla). If you love coasters, you'll love Magic Mountain's attractions—including *five* water rides.

Take your pick of the Apocalypse, Full Throttle, Scrambler, Road Runner Express, Tatsu, and more.

A LOCAL KID SAYS:
"Knott's Berry Farm is my favorite theme park because they have the best rides."
—Alex, 11

TELL THE ADULTS

It's often tough to eat healthy at theme parks, but Disney is making that easier. Kids' meals now include a healthy side of fruit or veggies and a choice of lowfat milk, juice, or water rather than a sugary drink. Toddler meals are also available in some places. If you don't see a kids' menu, just ask!

Californians who visit all the time often brown-bag it for lunch or dinner. It's cheaper and saves time! Always pack reusable water bottles and snacks.

There are a lot of restaurants just outside the parks in Downtown Disney, whether you want pizza, a sandwich, or to eat amid monkeys in a tropical rain forest at the Rainforest Cafe (1515 Disneyland Dr., Anaheim; 714-772-0413; rainforestcafe.com).

Especially if you want a character meal or a sit-down meal within the theme parks, it's smart to make a reservation ahead of time. (You can book up to 60 days in advance at 714-781-3463.)

Downtown Disney is a great place to shop—and trade pins—as the shops open early and close late.

You can also de-stress the experience by staying overnight at one of the Disney hotels so you can take advantage of early admission to the parks, take a break during the day for a swim—and a nap—and easily return in the evening for the fireworks.

Visit disneyland.disney.go.com for the latest deals on the three Disneyland Resort Hotels with their themed meals, amenities, and decor. Free transportation to and from the parks is available via monorails and trams and buses to neighboring hotels. There are more than 40 properties nearby known as Disneyland Good Neighbor hotels. Visit the Anaheim/Orange County Visitor and Convention Bureau at anaheimoc.org and go to "deals and discounts" or call 714-765-8888.

To further de-stress your theme park experience, take a virtual tour with the kids at disneyland .com before you visit and make sure everyone gets a pick each day of their "top attraction." Alternate whose attraction goes first each day!

Princess Power!

Disneyland is where many of the Disney princesses live, and you can become one, too, with sparkles in your hair, tiaras, wands, and dresses, or a "cool dude" prince at the Bibbidi Bobbidi Boutique. (Of course, this costs extra and you need reservations. It's in Fantasyland.) The boutique sells everything princess, and you can get your picture taken here too. You'll see lots of little girls in the park in their favorite princess's dress—including Belle, Jasmine, Mulan, Pocahontas, Tiana, Ariel, and Aurora. Who is your favorite princess?

At Fantasy Faire, you can meet and great your favorite princesses throughout the day. Walk through Sleeping Beauty's Castle, which will tell you her story, and try your hands at Scottish games while waiting to meet Princess Merida.

If you want to eat with your favorite princesses, you can at Ariel's Grotto in Disney California Adventure. Make sure your parents make reservations by calling 714-781-3463.

DID YOU KNOW?

There are 11 Disney princesses, in addition to Elsa and Anna from the Academy Award–winning *Frozen*. Snow White was the first. She made her debut in 1937 in *Snow White and the Seven Dwarfs*. Cinderella was the second in 1950.

USE THE SPACE BELOW TO DRAW PICTURES OF ANY CELEBRITIES OR DISNEY CHARACTERS YOU MIGHT SEE.

10

Disney California Adventure:
Coasters, Hang Gliding & Radiator Springs

Ready to race?

Radiator Springs Racers at **Disney California Adventure** (1313 S. Disneyland Dr., Anaheim; 714-781-4565; disney land.disney.go.com/disneys-california-adventure) is everyone's new favorite ride. You really will feel like you are in "the cutest little town in Carburetor Country" where all the characters of the *Cars* movies live.

California Adventure has some of the Disneyland Resort's most popular attractions. You'll love **Soarin' Over California,** which makes you feel as if you are hang gliding over the state—from Yosemite Falls to an aircraft carrier in San Diego Bay to San Francisco's Golden Gate Bridge.

DID YOU KNOW?

The entrance to Disney California Adventure is Buena Vista Street, which is designed to look like the Los Angeles Walt Disney saw when he first arrived in 1923. He was just 22 years old and had only $40 in his pocket.

Everything in this park is themed after California, from the entrance designed to look like 1920s L.A. when Walt Disney arrived to Hollywoodland to Paradise Pier, which is supposed to make you think of old-fashioned California seaside boardwalks, to Grizzly Peak, an 8-acre mini wilderness like Northern California's redwood country.

Coaster lovers give a thumbs up to **California Screamin',** the centerpiece of Paradise Pier. It's designed to look like an old-fashioned wooden coaster, but the thrills are all 21st century. The cars go from zero to 55 miles per hour in less than 5 seconds!

We can't forget **The Twilight Zone Tower of Terror.** According to legend, lightning struck the building on Halloween night 1939, and an entire guest wing disappeared— along with an elevator carrying five people. Are you ready for the biggest drop of your life?

A LOCAL KID SAYS:
"My favorite ride at California Adventure is California Screamin'."
—Jared, 12

Of course, every ride at California Adventure isn't scary! If you want to get wet, head for **Grizzly River Run.** Check out the mining relics scattered about and get ready to get drenched on your raft.

Everyone loves **Toy Story Midway Mania!** You wear 3-D glasses and try to see how many points you can score on the animated targets. You are inside the Midway. It is really cool! And when you are done, check out the Paradise Pier Midway with plenty of games.

At **Turtle Talk with Crush,** everyone's favorite cartoon turtle actually talks to you, answering questions. Even if you don't watch the Muppets anymore on TV, you'll laugh along with them at **Muppet Vision 3-D.**

A VISITING KID SAYS:
"I liked Soarin' Over California. It is really realistic, and you'll feel like you are really hang gliding."
—Marie Claire, 13, Arkansas

You won't want to miss the It's Tough to be A Bug Show either with plenty of creepy-crawlies and 4-D effects.

Cars Land is the newest addition to California Adventure complete with a 525-foot-long Route 66. Stop for a shake at Flo's V8 Cafe and check out all the neon lights after dark. Board one of Luigi's flying tires (think bumper cars meet flying saucers), and then get ready to compete against other race cars as you drive through Ornament Valley, meeting the *Cars* crew along the way. Wow! That was some hairpin turn!

A LOCAL KID SAYS:
"If you like thrills, go to the Tower of Terror—if you don't go on anything else!"
—Gaelan, 11

{ **What's Cool?** Watching the nighttime water and lights show World of Color water-side. There are 1,200 fountains. Get there 45 minutes ahead of time for a good spot!

Pin Mania!

Wherever you go at Disney California Adventure, you'll see adults and kids wearing lanyards around their necks that are covered with shiny pins. There are hundreds of different ones! You can buy a pin to commemorate your birthday or your favorite ride, character, or Disney movie (disneystore.com). There are light-up pins, pins that spin, and 3-D pins.

The Walt Disney Company has always offered collectible Disney pins. During the Millennium Celebration in 1999, they encouraged guests to trade pins, and today, many grown-ups and kids do at the parks and even on eBay.

Want to start trading? Find a Disney pin you like and look for a Disney cast member wearing a pin lanyard. They're ready to trade!

A VISITING KID SAYS:
"I love collecting Disney pins. I have over 90 so far."
—Macy, 11, Orange, CT

Holidays with Mickey

It seems Mickey and Minnie are always celebrating something. Some of the most fun celebrations—besides your own birthday, of course:

- FOURTH OF JULY: Celebrate Independence Day with especially cool fireworks.

- HALLOWEEN: At Disneyland, Halloween Time lets you celebrate in not too scary ways with special shows, fireworks, and Mickey's Halloween Party.

- CHRISTMAS: By early November, you'll see the holiday decorations on Main Street. There's a special holiday-themed fireworks show, A Christmas Fantasy parade, and more.

DID YOU KNOW?

You can see a model of Rock Candy Mountain, an attraction Walt Disney designed but never built, in the window of Trolley Treats in California Adventure.

TELL THE ADULTS

If anyone in the family has special needs or challenges, Disney California Adventure has a special Guide Map for Guests with Disabilities, special handheld devices that verbally describe the parks, and assistive listening devices as well as special accommodations for those with autism and other challenges (disneyland.disney.go.com/plan/guest-services/guests-with-disabilities).

Toy Story Midway Mania! and Soarin' Over California have particularly devoted fans. Get to the park early and get to these attractions first to take advantage of the FASTPASS system whenever you

{ **What's Cool?** Soarin' Over California. Get a FASTPASS for this ride as soon as you get to the park; it's one of California Adventure's most popular attractions. Try to sit in the first row.

can to avoid waiting in line. There is also a lot of entertainment at the park that won't require waits:

Red Car News Boys where Mickey Mouse joins the fun at the Buena Vista Street's Red Car Trolley.

Phineas and Ferb's Rockin' Rollin' Dance Party where you can dance along.

Pixar Play Parade.

World of Color 25-minute night show of music animation and special effects all over water.

DID YOU KNOW?

You can draw your own favorite character and learn how animation works at Disney Animation and the Animation Academy at Disney California Adventure.

Staying Safe

Theme parks are big places. Set up a meeting place just in case some of you get separated. Have your parents write down the name of your hotel, the phone number, and their cell phone numbers in case you get separated (sure you know their cell number—but in case you forget). If you do get separated from your parents, look for someone in a Disney uniform. They can help you find your family!

Put your name and contact numbers on your cameras and backpacks. Disney does a great job of returning lost items.

And don't try to stand on tiptoe to meet the height requirements of a ride. They are there for a reason— to keep you safe!

DID YOU KNOW?

James Marshall discovered gold at Sutter's Sawmill in Coloma in 1848. It would lead to the famous Gold Rush of 1849. People came from all over the country, hoping to get rich. (That's where the term "49ers" first came from.)

ADVENTURE SCAVENGER HUNT

Look carefully in the park for all the following and check off what you find!

- ☐ The Golden Gate Bridge
- ☐ Yosemite
- ☐ California Screamin'
- ☐ Tower of Terror
- ☐ Grizzly River Run
- ☐ Woody and Buzz
- ☐ Crush
- ☐ Kermit
- ☐ Bugs
- ☐ Minnie Mouse
- ☐ Someone wearing a lanyard with shiny pins
- ☐ Someone winning a game in the Midway
- ☐ A replica of Walt Disney
- ☐ Lightning McQueen
- ☐ Paradise Pier
- ☐ A visitor taking a silly picture

USE THE SPACE BELOW TO COLLECT SIGNATURES OF ANY CELEBRITIES OR DISNEY CHARACTERS YOU MIGHT SEE.

What a Trip!

I came to San Diego with:

_____

_____

_____

The weather was:

_____

_____

_____

We went to:

_____

_____

_____

We ate:

_____

_____

_____

We bought:

_____

_____

_____

I saw these famous San Diego sites:

_____

_____

_____

My favorite thing about San Diego was:

_____

_____

_____

My best memory of San Diego was:

_____

_____

_____

My favorite souvenir is:

_____

_____

_____

WHAT DID YOU SEE?

You had such a great time in San Diego! Draw some pictures or paste in some photos of your trip!

Index

Answer Keys

Secret Word Decoder (p. 30)
Balboa Carousel

Know Your Sea Animals (p. 61)
C	beluga whale
E	Asian small-clawed otter
B	green sea turtle
D	manatee
A	manta ray

Word Search: Talk Like a Surfer (p. 75)

T	A	K	I	N	G	G	A	S	B	V	M	S
A	L	A	B	V	R	S	U	V	S	E	T	O
B	L	S	M	R	E	O	E	U	E	G	Q	A
E	T	R	O	B	M	A	R	P	O	P	U	P
R	I	E	C	T	M	A	B	N	A	H	I	R
U	M	A	N	L	I	E	R	R	R	T	V	F
B	E	T	Q	L	E	C	S	T	O	K	E	D
X	B	A	Z	B	O	N	H	M	N	S	R	S
M	R	R	Y	O	C	C	O	L	A	E	G	S
Q	N	I	O	R	A	H	U	M	L	T	R	B
Y	F	O	G	N	A	R	L	Y	N	C	W	O
J	U	S	M	S	O	C	D	N	A	L	G	M
E	C	V	Y	T	N	R	E	E	W	R	E	B
B	A	I	L	M	E	U	R	O	N	I	C	A

LEGOLAND

Fill in the Missing Letters (p. 99)

1) Castle Hill

2) Dino Island

3) DUPLO Village

4) Fun Town

4) Imagination Zone

6) Land of AdvenTure

7) Miniland USA

8) Pirate Shores

What Are the Parts of a Plant That We Eat? (p. 113)

Root–Carrot

Stem–Asparagus

Leaves–Lettuce

Flower–Broccoli

Fruit–Tomato

Seed–Sunflower Seeds

Answer: The four things that all plants need to survive are Sun, Soil, Water, and Air.

About the Author

Award-winning author Eileen Ogintz is a leading national family travel expert whose syndicated Taking the Kids is the most widely distributed column in the country on family travel. She has also created TakingtheKids.com, which helps families make the most of their vacations together. Ogintz is the author of seven family travel books and is often quoted in major publications such as *USA Today*, the *Wall Street Journal*, and the *New York Times*, as well as parenting and women's magazines on family travel. She has appeared on such television programs as *The Today Show*, *Good Morning America*, and *The Oprah Winfrey Show*, as well as dozens of local radio and television news programs. She has traveled around the world with her three children and others in the family, talking to traveling families wherever she goes. She is also the author of *The Kid's Guide to New York City*, *The Kid's Guide to Orlando*, *The Kid's Guide to Washington, DC*, *The Kid's Guide to Chicago*, *The Kid's Guide to Los Angeles*, and *The Kid's Guide to Boston* (Globe Pequot Press).